FOR GOD
—— AND ——
SPAIN

The truth about the Spanish war

HUGH DE BLÁCAM

FOR GOD
—AND—
SPAIN

THE TRUTH ABOUT THE SPANISH WAR

HUGH DE BLÁCAM

CRUACHAN
HILL PRESS

Nihil Obstat:

CAROLUS DOYLE, S.J.
Censor Librorum
Dublin, Ireland

Imprimatur:

+EDUARDUS BYRNE
Archiep. Dublinen, Hiberniae Primas.
DUBLINI, die 3 Octobris, 1936.

Copyright © 2022 Cruachan Hill Press

The main text of this work is in the public domain. All other material is all rights reserved—it may not be reproduced, transmitted, or stored in any form by any means—electronic, mechanical, recorded, photocopy, or otherwise–without prior written permission from the author, except for brief excerpts in articles or critical reviews.

ISBN: 978-1-957206-10-3
Cover Art by Jessica Fellmeth

Published by
Cruachan Hill Press
12552 E Michigan Ave.
Grass Lake, MI 49240
www.cruachanhill.com

Printed and Bound in the United States of America

CONTENTS

Introduction	1
Foreword	9
1. Civil War Begins	11
2. The Terror of July	14
3. The Course of the War	18
4. The Historical Causes	22
5. The Outbreak	33
6. Issues at Stake: The Left	38
7. Issues at Stake: The Right	41
8. The War Described	44
9. What is Fascism?	49
10. Some Charges Answered	52
11. What is Our Part?	58
Appendix	60

INTRODUCTION

THE SPANISH CIVIL WAR was already the subject of an intense propaganda campaign immediately upon its outbreak in 1936. The international press, was largely sympathetic to the Second Republic, portraying the nationalist resistance as an insurrection against a peaceful democratic government. The conflict between Francisco Franco and President Manuel Azaña's Popular Front was framed as a coup of authoritarian fascism against tolerant democracy. The Left castigated the Catholic Church endlessly as the instigator of the conflict. The cover image of this book, for example, was propagandized by the Left as proof of clerical aggression. It is nothing of the sort; this image actually depicts seminarians in Pamplona fulfilling their basic compulsory military training under Spanish law. It dates from 1922, years before the hostilities of the war. But facts be damned, as the narrative of freedom fighters taking on a repressive Church was too salacious for progressive propagandists to pass up.

Then, as now, the media grossly oversimplified the situation. The Second Republic of the 1930s was anything but tolerant. The Red Terror (a campaign of wanton murder and destruction levelled against Catholics and supporters of the nationalists) began in 1934 in Asturias with the mass killing of 37 priests and destruction of 58 churches. The string of butchery continued for two years *before* the civil war even began. It was only after two years of terror at the hands of government-aligned Leftist death squads—culminating in the assassination of Calvo Sotelo in the summer of 1936—that the nationalists under Franco took up arms against the Madrid government.

Misinformation about the Spanish Civil War continues to this day, with most popular content about the war exhibiting a decidedly pro-Republican slant. Of course, Franco's acquiescence to the use of Nazi airpower to destroy Republican targets makes him an easy punching bag, as does Franco's ideological alignment with the Fascist movements of Italy, Portugal, and elsewhere. But to get to the truth about the Spanish Civil War, we must move beyond guilt-by-association to understand the real causes, events, and actors of this tumultuous period.

This was the purpose behind Hugh de Blácam's creation of this little book in 1936. Hugh de Blácam (1891-1951) was an English-born Irish author, journalist, and editor. Though raised in a deeply Protestant Ulster family, he adopted Irish nationalism and was affiliated with Sinn Féin, the Fianna Fáil, and Clann na Poblachta. In London he joined the Gaelic League, where he was exposed to the writings of G.K. Chesterton, converting to Catholicism as a result. Shortly thereafter, de Blácam then returned home to Ireland to offer his support to the Irish nationalists

INTRODUCTION

during the uprising of 1919, for which he was briefly incarcerated by the British. After Irish independence he worked as a journalist for the *Irish Times* and was editor of the *Catholic Standard*.

Though initially enamored with socialism, de Blácam would become a vocal supporter of Catholic social teaching as found in Leo XIII's *Rerum Novarum*. In his economics, de Blácam was a corporatist, eschewing both Capitalism and Communism. He reserved his fiercest vitriol for Communism, however, which he accurately perceived as a kind of anti-civilization: destructive of family, property, culture, and religion. This naturally engendered in him sympathy for Europe's various Fascist movements, which were at that time the only forces capable of resisting Communism. Though de Blácam deplored the heavy-handed tactics of men like Franco and Mussolini (the latter of whom he complained was "not Catholic enough"), he never ceased promoting the ideal of an integrated Catholic state. De Blácam turned rather to men of milder mettle for his inspiration, like Austria's Engelbert Dollfuss and Portugal's António de Oliveira Salazar.

When civil war broke out in Spain in July of 1936, de Blácam lent his pen to the cause of Spanish Catholics, whom the media were already portraying as the instigators of the violence. The result was this book, *For God and Spain: The Truth About the Spanish War*. The title is slightly misleading, for his book is not a history of the war itself (it was published only a few months into the conflict). Rather, it is about the history of the events that led up to the war. In reviewing this history, the purpose of de Blácam's book is three-fold (i) to exonerate Catholic nationalists of the stigma that they instigated the conflict (ii) to shed light on

FOR GOD AND SPAIN

Hugh de Blácam (1891-1951)

INTRODUCTION

the atrocities committed by the Communists, whom de Blácam identifies as the true aggressors, and (iii) to elicit support from Catholics abroad for the plight of their Spanish brethren.

Lest we are at this point tempted to roll our eyes in supposing we are about to read a glowing apologia for Francoist Fascism, we should note that de Blácam is reserved in his praise of Franco. He openly expresses disapproval of Franco's methods and does not relish violence, even wielded in a just cause. De Blácam is not concerned with promoting the Falangist movement so much as supporting Spanish Catholics and opposing the advance of Communism. To the degree that he supports Franco, it is as a means to this end. He lavishes much greater praise on Gil Robles (1898-1980), leader of the Spanish Confederation of the Autonomous Right (CEDA), a conservative Catholic party and the largest bloc in the Cortes, the Spanish parliament. De Blácam calls Robles "the ablest and wisest democratic statesmen of Europe" and "the hope of Spain." As leader of the majority party from 1933 to 1936, Gil Robles tried to stabilize the political situation in Spain through purely political means but lacked the iron will to successfully beat down the Communists. De Blácam portrays him as a man too principled to fight back against the low blows offered by the Left. "The accepted rules of parliamentary democracy were observed, with Quixotic honor by the leader of the Right," he says of Robles, while "they were broken by the President of the Republic, under pressure from the Left." For de Blácam, Robles is like a man who loses a bout because he insists on fighting fair even when his opponent is fighting dirty.

This is an essential piece of de Blácam's apologia, as it frames the Francoist movement as essentially defensive. Faced with the brutal onslaught of the Red Terror and the impotence of the Right to do anything through the political process, Spanish Catholics had no choice but to embrace Franco as the only force with the will and means to protect them from Communist violence. The Catholic cause is thus taken up into the cause of Franco and legitimized, while the Madrid government is delegitimized due to its acquiescence to—if not support of—the Red Terror. De Blácam thus flips the popular narrative on its head.

Hugh de Blácam's presentation of the facts is certainly not perfect. He wrote in the fall of 1936 when details about the chaotic events of July-August were still emerging. Certain deeds—like the nationalist massacre of civilians at Badajoz in August 1936—were intentionally obscured by the perpetrators, the facts only emerging later. For example, de Blácam assures us that those killed at Badajoz were only done so after being convicted at a trial as being part of irregular Communist forces. History has subsequently demonstrated that the vast majority of dead at Badajoz were civilians, executed summarily with no trial, mowed down by mounted machine guns for no other crime than being residents of a Republican-aligned city. Given the deliberate attempts of the Francoists to obfuscate what occurred at Badajoz, however, we can hardly blame de Blácam for this. His writing thus comes with the benefits— and shortcomings—of one who is commenting on current events as they unfold without benefit of historical hindsight.

This is the real value in de Blácam's little book, that it gives us a glimpse into the way conservative Catholics of the 1930s viewed the events unfolding in Spain. From a

INTRODUCTION

historical standpoint, it is of inestimable value that de Blácam chose to include lengthy excerpts from the Vatican paper *L'Osservatore Romano* in Chapters 8 and 11, as well as a transcript of Pope Pius XI's radio broadcast of September 14, 1936. These passages offer clear insight into the mind of Rome on the civil war from important sources that have tended to be overlooked in considerations of this subject.

Though it falls short of an exhaustive chronicle of the Spanish Civil War, de Blácam's book does an admirable job of laying out the arguments for Catholic support of the nationalist movement while simultaneously demonstrating that the Catholics who took up arms in 1936 for God and for Spain did so in self-defense. When de Blácam wrote in fall of 1936, the long expanse of Franco's reign was yet to come, and despite his misgivings about the man, de Blácam viewed him as the only chance Spain had to stave off a total Bolshevik takeover. "Whether Franco acted in the best of ways, or whether he is perfectly sincere," de Blácam says, "it is a truth beyond yea or nay that Western civilization will perish if he fails."

PHILLIP CAMPBELL
October 4, 2022
Feast of St. Francis of Assisi

FOREWORD

SPEAKING by radio from Castel Gandolfo on September 14th, 1936, Our Holy Father, Pius XI, told the people of Spain and the whole world how the heart of the Vicar of Christ grieves in the grief of Spain and glories in the glory of those who have suffered there for God. His Holiness, in words of such eloquence as seemed to come from the very soul of the Church, blessed those "who have taken upon them the difficult and dangerous task of restoring the law of God and the rights of conscience," and counselled them to do all things in charity and without wrath; the Holy Father blessed also the willful ones who are also his children but have turned their hands to dreadful acts, pleading with them to return to the ways of brotherhood with their nation and peace with all men.

In the essay that follows, the writer has tried to set forth the solid historical truth of the outbreak and of the purposes of the Insurgents. He has tried not to labor the awful wrongs done by the revolutionaries, whose works provoked the Rising, and, by giving only a brief summary of the proven atrocities against God and civilization, has understated the immensity of the wrongs done. This moderation—and refraining from stress on the magnitude of the terror—is in harmony, the writer hopes, with the Church's mind, as shown us by the Holy Father, wishing for peace only less than for justice and Christian order.

The facts given can all be attested by evidence, though it is true that they have been largely suppressed by most of the newspapers of the English-using world, owing to influences, political, spiritual or opportunist which one does not care to specify here and now. Let all who read, read with awe and not with anger, praying for the victory of the good cause and for mercy and reconciliation among the people of noble Spain. Let all remember that Spain is fighting for the cause of all Christendom when its soldiers strive to hold back the atheistic materialism of Moscow, and the church-burning, culture-destroying fury. For the freedom of our Faith, and for the life of our own grave, Christian civilization, the parties of the Right and their soldiers are waging the Last Crusade.

Hugh de Blácam
FEAST OF THE EXALTATION OF THE CROSS, 1936

I. CIVIL WAR BEGINS

ONE EVENING in July when folk came in from the hayfields for tea, the wireless news said: "A Spanish Statesman, Calvo Sotelo, has been found murdered in Madrid." That was the first dread news to warn us that the long tension in Spain was to break in a terrific social war. Fuller tidings next day told how Calvo Sotelo, one of the principal leaders of the Conservative groups in the Cortes, or Parliament, had been arrested at his home by Government agents, and then had been murdered.[1]

On the same night, the dwelling of Gil Robles, the principal leader of the Conservative groups, also had been visited in like manner, but he had been absent—he had flown and escaped. At the funeral, Gil Robles appeared. He

---

[1] José Calvo Sotelo, 1st Duke of Calvo Sotelo (1893-1936). Spanish jurist and politician, Minister of Finance during the dictatorship of Miguel Primo de Rivera and a leading figure during the Second Republic. He was assassinated by the bodyguard of Socialist party leader Indalecio Prieto. His death was the immediate prelude to the Spanish Civil War.

José Calvo Sotelo (1893-1936). His assassination on July 13, 1936 was the immediate catalyst of the Spanish Civil War.

CIVIL WAR BEGINS

charged the Government with responsibility for the death of Calvo Sotelo and for the series of outrages that had led up to that crime. Those for whom he spoke, he said, after long and patient effort to co-operate with the Government in maintaining constitutional rule, found themselves baffled. The Government itself had destroyed constitutional ways.

Two days later, on July 17, Gil Robles had fled for his life from the terror-stricken capital. News came that the army in Morocco had renounced its allegiance to the Madrid Government. Throughout Spain, army garrisons rose in like manner. There was, in brief, a general military revolt, headed by General Franco, who was in charge of the chief body of the Spanish army, then stationed in Morocco. Hideous turmoil followed which we must contemplate before we go on to see how the war developed and then examine the causes of the conflict in detail.[2]

---

[2] The rebels were strong in Morocco. Most troops were local *regulares* and majority Muslim. They had been told that the Madrid government intended to forbid the worship of Allah.

II. THE TERROR OF JULY

THE AGRICULTURAL regions welcomed the insurgent armies and their cause, and so more than half Spain at once was lost to Madrid.[3] Most of the navy, much of the air force, and parts of some garrisons, however, remained loyal to the Madrid Government. So did a great part of the populace in the great industrial cities, particularly Barcelona, that big rich, revolutionary center, capital of the self-governing region of Catalonia.

The Government distributed arms to the social revolutionary organizations, which include trade unions, and a Red militia thus sprung into being in a day. This militia was hurled upon the insurgent garrisons in Madrid, Barcelona and other places where the insurgents had not yet prevailed. The garrisons fell in these two cities, but held in others, such as Toledo.

In effect, the Government had armed the mob. Let us understand what the organizations were, to which the

---

[3] Predominantly in the south and east.

THE TERROR OF JULY

arms were served out. They were, as we have said, revolutionary trade unions. Some of the unions are Socialistic, some Bolshevistic, but two of the most important, known as the F.A.I. and C.N.T. go even further than Russia—they are Anarchist.[4] There is in Spain a vast group of revolutionaries who follow the doctrine of Bakhunin, who said that the State and all other institutions of authority ought to be destroyed.[5] Factories, villages, men, all should be a law to themselves. Morality no longer would exist. The Anarchists and Communists held Barcelona and other places, yielding only a formal allegiance to Madrid. They have seized their own anarchic power and are leagued together only for the destruction of religion and order.

Such are the trade unions that the Nationalists intend to suppress. In action, they are the mob armed. Awful scenes of revolutionary violence followed the rise of these destructive forces where they prevailed. Murder and massacre, sacrilege and arson, were seen on the greatest scale of Western history. Now, mark this: the chief fury of the Red hosts was wreaked on the Church: the Church was seized upon as the enemy, and bishops and priests who failed to escape into hiding were slaughtered.

Barcelona is the most hideous example of this outburst of hatred for holy things. There, the insurgent garrison was in a hopeless position from the outset; for it

---

[4] F.A.I. (Federación Anarquista Ibérica; Iberian Anarchist Federation); C.N.T. (Confederación Nacional del Trabajo; National Confederation of Labor).

[5] Mikhail Alexandrovich Bakunin (1814-1876) was a Russian revolutionary anarchist, socialist, and the founder of collectivist anarchism.

was in unfriendly country by reason of the Catalan racial feeling. It was small, and weak and gave up the fight in a few hours. Forthwith, however, the victorious Reds poured through the city of which they were the undisputed masters, travelling in vehicles that bore the emblems of their Union, the C.N.T. and F.A.I., and. they burnt every Catholic church in that vast city save two.

One of Europe's most ancient and splendid historic shrines was but one among the scores of churches that were reduced, in a few hours, to smoking ruins. The number of priests murdered in this festival of hate was 400 in Barcelona alone. A striking example of the savagery was this: the coffins of nuns were dug up and opened, and the bodies of the long dead holy women were put on show in the streets with hideous results. Dead Carmelite monks were exposed in the same manner along the outer wall of the church.

What happened in Barcelona was on a bigger scale than elsewhere; but not more horrible. Five bishops were murdered at the outset—those of Barbasto, Siguenza, Jaen, Segovia and Lerida.[6] At the town of Deimiel, thirty-one Passionists were slain; two Franciscan communities were put to death, and eighteen Christian brothers. Elsewhere a community of St. John of God Brothers (men engaged in the humblest and most unselfish of social works) was massacred, and in another place eighty Augustinian were

---

[6] The episcopal dead were Bl. Florentino Asensio Barroso, Bishop of Barbasto; Eustaquio Nieto y Martín, Bishop of Siguenza, after whose death the see remained vacant until 1944; Manuel Basulto y Jiménez, Bishop of Jaen; Bl. Salvi Huix Miralpéix, Bishop of Lerida. Regarding the Diocese of Segovia, de Blácam errs by confusing Segovia with Segorbe. It was Bishop Miguel de los Santos Serra y Sucarrats of Segobe who was killed in the summer of 1936.

put to death. Outrages against nuns were many, and too horrible to relate. The complete tale of slaughter of these unresisting religious is known only to Heaven.[7]

In the weeks that followed, in the ruthless civil war, it became the rule on each side to shoot the officers of surrendering parties. The Reds, we are told by Mr. L. T. Fleming of the *Irish Times*, who visited the battlefields of Aragon under their protection, shot all priests with the officers. Dreadful sacrilege was wrought on the Divine Presence of the altar. Libraries were destroyed, together with priceless works of art, for no reason save hatred of their Catholic associations. Such was the Red Terror, wherever the Madrid Government prevailed. Mass could not be said in the Capital, or in Barcelona, or in any place remaining in Red control.

---

[7] At the time of publication, 498 martyrs of the Spanish Civil War have been beatified. The total number of dead is estimated at 6,800 clergy and religious.

III. THE COURSE OF THE WAR

FROM the start, General Franco was master of Morocco, where the main body of the regular Spanish army was stationed. At home, General Mola, at Burgos, was quickly master of the North of Spain, save for the Basque provinces, which were temporarily neutral, pending a settlement of their local demands and the coastline. Hosts of young volunteers of the Falange Espanola, a Fascist league, joined his standard at Burgos. In the South, General Queipo de Llano mastered Andalusia. The insurgent air force overcame the navy, and Franco was able to bring over thousands of regular troops and plentiful war material.

With these resources at his disposal, Franco won a sea base at Huelva and advanced on Badajoz on the Portuguese border, taking it after a big struggle—the first big victory of the war. Soon the insurgents held a line, with a railway behind it, running in a great curve across Spain: Huelva-Badajoz-Salamanca-Valladolid-Burgos, and, after the second big victory of the war, Irún. All behind this line,

THE COURSE OF THE WAR

Generalissimo Francisco Franco (1892-1975), leader of the Nationalist forces during the Civil War and future ruler of Spain from 1936 to 1975.

save some isolated strongholds, became insurgent country, with friendly Portugal behind it. From it, they pressed forward on Madrid from the West. In the ensuing struggle, their advance was steady everywhere save where Catalonia's Red forces held a line against them in the northeast.[8]

Franco met Mola at Burgos.[9] There, after Mass at the historic cathedral, they prayed together at the tomb of El Cid Campeador, the hero who from Burgos began the liberation of Christian Spain long ago. A military Government was set up, with General Cabanallas at its head, and Gil Robles came to Burgos from his refuge in Portugal to announce his support of what was done.

At Seville, on the feast of the Assumption, Cardinal Ilundain blessed the old red-and-gold flag of Spain, and General Queipo de Llano unfurled it.[10] The mayor of the city said that the tri-colour flag of the Republic never had been more than a party emblem, but the historic national flag would symbolize the well-being of all. In contrast to this course by the patriots, the Madrid Government resigned after the fall of Irún, and a new Government, openly Communistic, was formed by Senor Largo Caballero, founder of Communist Youth—one of the organizations which took a main part in the destruction of churches. At the same time (the beginning of September) President

---

[8] Hueva was taken on July 27-29, 1936. Badajoz fell on August 14 and became the scene of a frightful massacre by the Francoists, earning General Juan Yagüe the nickname "Butcher of Bajadoz."

[9] Emilio Mola y Vidal, 1st Duke of Mola (1887-1937), one of the three principal leaders of the Nationalist coup.

[10] Variations of the red and gold had been used from 1785 to 1927, when the Second Republic abandoned it for one of red, yellow, and murrey (dark purple).

THE COURSE OF THE WAR

Azalia welcomed the Russian Ambassador and exchanged assurances of fraternity between Madrid and Moscow.

Thus, whatever the merits of the case at the beginning, when confused statements were made about the ideas governing each side, the war quickly became defined as one between Nationalism and Catholicism on one side, and Bolshevism and Atheism on the other. Wherever the insurgents have prevailed—and they were masters of three-quarters of Spain by the first week of September—the Crucifix is restored to the schools. Everywhere that Madrid rules, the schools are under an atheist whom Largo Caballero has made his Minister of Public Instruction.

IV. THE HISTORICAL CAUSES

WE WILL consider now how this war between Communism and Christian civilization came about; and for this we must notice the main heads of Spanish history and the events which forced the conflict to take the form of war.

(A) *Past History.*—In the age when the Protestant Reformation broke up the unity of Christendom, Spain was the principal champion of the historic Catholic order. At that time, her national spirit, raised high by the patriot monarchs Ferdinand and Isabella, was united to a grand religious fervor. Her mariners sought out America and her monks went with them to found those great new Christian nations which now occupy South America; the track of those builders of civilization is seen on the American map up to San Francisco and Santa Fe. At that same time, the Spanish fleet in the Mediterranean were guarding Europe from the hosts of Islam, while scholars and saints and mystics abounded in her universities and monasteries, and the Jesuits were sending out those missions to the East which won hundreds of thousands of souls. For a century, Spain was the powerhouse of the Catholic world, and her mighty works were done by men who poured out blood and wealth and zeal and life in the selfless spirit of sacrifice. Save the vast Irish missions to the Continent in the Dark Ages, no such other vast outpouring of Christian service ever has been seen. This prodigious spending of energy exhausted Spain (as Ireland of old was exhausted); for Nature has made Spain poor, and such works could not be maintained from her resources for ever. So Spain sank into a rest that lasted for more than two centuries, while other parts of Europe were gathering worldly power and wealth. She was backward, materially speaking, when her national spirit began to revive in the last century. The land lacked irrigation to make it fruitful, and easy-going aristocrats allowed their people to toil along in the old-fashioned ways not fitted for the stress of this age. Commerce and industry flourished in one region—Catalonia, with the great Mediterranean port of Barcelona as its capital, the Belfast of Spain. In Catalonia, a separate dialect is spoken (Catalan), and social revolutionary ideas are allied to a semi-national feeling.

(B) *The Monarchy Falls.*—The revival of Spanish energy in the last half 19th century took two forms. There were men like the great national teacher, Menendez y Pelayo, who cried to the nation to build a new greatness on its noble Christian tradition.[11] There were others, like the noted Blasco Ibafiez, who directed the reviving energy to

---

[11] Menendez y Pelayo (1856-1912), a Spanish scholar, historian and literary critic who was nominated for the Nobel Prize in literature five times.

destruction.[12] These wanted to throw down monarchy and Church and the Christian family and to build a new, Godless State. In 1923, the agitation by anarchists and others of the destructive side led to the murder of the Cardinal Archbishop of Saragossa.[13] In the wild disorder of the time, General Primo de Rivera, with King Alfonso's approval, formed a Military Directory, and Parliament was suspended. The Directory lasted eight years. During that time, the land had peace. Primo de Rivera, a devout Christian gentleman, set about reforms that were wholly admirable. He began by purging the services of idlers; he overhauled the national finances and made the administration efficient. He enforced moral reforms that cleaned the cities. He set about big material works, such as the building of railways into regions that still were poor through isolation, and the harnessing of waterpower. Grand exhibitions were held at Seville and Barcelona, which displayed the nation's resources. Trans-Atlantic flights were organized which showed the new Spain's power. Spain made more material progress in his time than in any modern period, and he has been described as the greatest Spanish statesman since Ferdinand and Isabella.

Unhappily, however, this noble and gentle statesman failed to complete his work, as he intended, by the establishment of a popular constitution. He was frustrated by a group of shiftless aristocrats who were unwilling to make the sacrifices that he demanded in order to put an end to agrarian grievances. The King is blamed for supporting them. Primo de Rivera was not a man of

---

[12] Vicente Blasco Ibáñez (1867-1928), a prolific writer, journalist, and politician.
[13] **Cardinal** Juan Soldevilla y Romero (1843-1923).

THE HISTORICAL CAUSES

Mussolini's overbearing kind, and he failed to assert his will. He had not raised an army of young political enthusiasts like the Fascisti of Italy. He advised, was overborne, and gave way. He offended the King and was dismissed—very ungratefully— to die of overwork and disappointment, in 1930. He was buried in the Carmelite habit. His fall was the tragedy of splendid intentions broken by too kindly a nature.

There is ample proof that the Directory was popular, but what Primo de Rivera won was lost by his successor, General Berenguer, a soldier picked by the King, good-natured, but lacking ability as well as strength. The ruling powers sank into inertia, but not so the revolutionary forces. In August 1930, the Republicans, Socialists, Communists, and other opposition groups met at San Sebastian and pledged themselves to a mutual truce while they worked unitedly for the overthrow of the monarchy. This was the first appearance of what is called now a United Front. The King blundered and called in the most inflexible of conservative politicians. In April 1931, local elections were called, and the politicians of the San Sabastian Pact triumphed in all the cities. Now, mark this: that 22,000 seats were held by Royalists and less than 6,000 were taken by Republicans. Furthermore, these 6,000 seats represented parties which had nothing in common save enmity to the Crown. However, since these seats were almost all in the cities, the election amounted to a sweeping urban revolution. There was uproar in Madrid and the King fled. The Republic was proclaimed by the urban minority.

(C) *How the Republic Fared.*—A Provisional Government was set up with a Liberal politician, Alcala Zamora, as Prime Minister. The leading figures, all members of the Pact, included men as diverse as Lerroux, a Liberal; Largo Caballero, a revolutionary Socialist; and Manuel Azaña, a bitter anti-Catholic, who became Prime Minister when Zamora became President. This mixed group—most of whom were Freemasons—enacted Liberal and Socialistic measures, confiscated the wealth of the Church, secularized education, and suppressed that Order which has done most for Spanish glory in the past, and in recent times had done enormous works of education that the State itself neglected, the Society of Jesus. An effort was made to socialize the land. A government which was erected on hate, was divided within itself, and assailed traditions and faith dear as life to Catholics, naturally failed to bring peace. In contrast to the Directory, the Republic saw strikes, riots, suppression of newspapers, internments, almost ceaselessly. In 1932, there was a military revolt by General Sanjurjo, which failed, and a few months later a revolt by Communists and Anarchists. Then, in April 1933, elections were held again, the first to be held on a true Republican base. What happened? The parties of the Right won 217 seats; the Centre, 162, and the Left only 93. The Right represented Catholics, Agrarians and some Monarchists; the Centre the Liberals and Moderate Republicans. The Liberal leader, Lerroux, now replaced the destructive Azaña as Premier, with Gil Robles, the principal Catholic statesman of the Right supporting him. This was a Coalition Government reflecting the true state of Spanish opinion.

(D) *The Rise of Gil Robles.*—Who was this Gil Robles, who now first appears in our story? He is one of the ablest and wisest democratic statesmen of Europe. The son of a noted Catholic scholar, he devoted his energies first to

THE HISTORICAL CAUSES

José María Gil-Robles y Quiñones de León (1898-1980), the leader of CEDA. His inability to stem the rising tide of Marxism led to the crisis of 1936.

Catholic Action.[14] He travelled the world, mastered political science, and strove through the great Catholic daily paper *El Debate* to inspire his nation with the ideals of Catholic social reform—the only principles which correct the wrongs of Capitalism without going over to the errors of Communism. Politics called him against his wish, but he quickly showed himself the greatest parliamentarian of the Republic. He offended the strong monarchists by announcing that he would work for reform within the Republic, refusing to question the status of the monarchy. Possibly, like most Spaniards not of revolutionary bent, he loves the tradition of the Crown; but he said that Spain was divided on that issue, and that what she needed was peace and Christian reform. C.E.D.A., the Confederation of Right Parties, made Gil Robles their chief, with Religion, Family, Fatherland, Social Order as their watchwords.[15] He became Minister of War under Lerroux and set about the reconstruction of the armed forces, while one of his colleagues, under his masterly direction, drew up a thorough scheme for agrarian reform, under which small ownership was to be multiplied, and farmers were to be lifted from depression by a sweeping correction of the prices of farm produce. For Gil Robles, agriculture is the main industry of Spain, on the prosperity of which the welfare of all others must be made to rest. Gil Robles did

---

[14] A loose association of groups of lay Catholics founded in 1922 who advocated for increased Catholic influence in society, especially in countries under anti-clerical regimes.

[15] Confederación Española de Derechas Autónomas, a conservative Catholic political party and heir to the earlier Catholic Acción Popular movement. CEDA insisted on a reformation of the republican constitution in favor of affirmation and defense of the principles of Christian civilization.

THE HISTORICAL CAUSES

not approve of the dictatorial system, though he had held a post under the Directory. Unlike Primo de Rivera, therefore, he gained the enthusiastic support of young men. He toured Spain by aeroplane, expounding his policy of Christian democratic reform, and the great cities welcomed him with enormous meetings. At Valencia he addressed what is said to have been the biggest political meeting ever held in Spain, and none were more in evidence than the young Catholic manhood of the South, even in that city which had been the anti-Christian Blasco Ibafiez' native place.

The rise of Gil Robles dismayed the powers of the Left. He was securing modifications of anti-clerical measures, and winning approval for a program of reform, not revolution. This meant good-bye to their destructive aims if it could not be checked, so they rose in arms. That was in October of 1934. The Catalan revolutionaries proclaimed Catalonia independent, there was an upheaval in Madrid and elsewhere, but chiefly in Asturias, where the miners were infected by the most violent ideas of Bolshevism. A hideous civil war raged, with several of the signatories of the Pact of San Sebastian siding against the Government of Lerroux, who was himself a signatory. The allies had split. Observe that the revolt was made against a duly elected majority Government. It was a deliberate effort of a defeated minority to gain its end at any ruthless cost. The true character of Bolshevism was shown in the anti-religious fury of the rebels. Many priests were killed in Oviedo. At Turón, not far distant, a community of De La Salle Brothers, with a Passionist priest, was martyred.[16] The

---

[16] The martyrs of Turón were a group eight members of the Institute of the Brothers of the Christian Schools, also known as De La

Government of Lerroux prevailed after a fortnight's hard fighting. In the crisis, Madrid was paralyzed, but organized Catholic youth, followers of Gil Robles, turned out and did the city's scavenging and distributed newspapers. Victory was a victory for the Right.

(E) *The Right is betrayed.*—It was obvious, when peace returned, that Gil Robles was the hope of Spain. In Parliament, however, he was not strong enough to prevail against the intrigues of enemies of the Faith. Lerroux was old and weak, he fell, and President Zamora sought to get a Government formed by one statesman after another out of the Centre parties. None was strong enough, yet still the President failed to invite the man who had proved his fitness. The latter months of 1935 were filled with crisis. A Fascist movement called the Spanish Phalanx sprang up, and young enthusiasts, led by Primo de Rivera's son, Don Jose, began to work for action as in Italy.[17] Conservative leaders of military type came to Gil Robles and begged him to call out the army and seize power. It is probable that most of the nation would have welcomed this action. The moment was favorable: the prestige of Gil Robles was at its height and the Left was lately defeated in arms. However, Gil Robles refused. It was at this time—the last months of 1935—that he made the tour we have mentioned, and it was at the prodigious and wildly enthusiastic meeting at Valencia that he publicly refused to take power by unconstitutional means. "We are asked," he said, "to carry

---

Salle Brothers, and one Passionist priest, executed in October 1934. They were canonized by John Paul II in 1999.

[17] More commonly known as the Falange Española. It later merged with Ramiro Ledesma's Juntas de Ofensiva Nacional-Sindicalista in 1934 to become the Falange Española de las JONS (FE de las JONS).

out a coup d'état. We will not: I will not forget my duty, nor will the Army forget its duty to proper authority. A coup d'état is for a defeated minority [he referred to the Communistic attempt of the year before] and not for a party that has the nation with it. We will take power when the time comes, from the hands of the nation. In the words of Cisneros: These are our powers, these are our army—the people of Spain!"

Yet still Zamora refused to invite the leader of the biggest single party in Parliament to form a Government. The accepted rules of parliamentary democracy were observed, with Quixotic honor by the leader of the Right; they were broken by the President of the Republic, under pressure from the Left, for fear of the Left. When all else failed and terrorism was breaking loose, the President suspended the Cortes. Democracy was baffled by the boasted Democrat! Then came the elections of February 1936, fought in the midst of fresh violence, simply and solely because the Right was to be denied what was its due.

(F) *The Fatal Election.*—The Allies of the Pact of 1930 came together again on the elections' eve and fought the election as the United Front.[18] The Crown was gone, but Christian conservation (if we may use the phrase) remained. Socialists, Communists, and Anarchists hated the prospect of a Catholic recovery more than they hated one another. The Right was less strongly united. The Fascists had been offended by the refusal of Gil Robles to seize power, and by his rebuke to their methods. The monarchists were lukewarm because he had refused to stand for a restoration.

---

[18] The *Frente Popular*, an electoral alliance formed January 1936 by various left-wing political organizations, instigated by Azaña in order to contest conservatives in that year's election.

These two groups, the Fascists (a growing number), and the monarchists, a considerable and influential body, stood aloof, convinced that the trickery which had baffled Gil Robles in parliament made support of his methods futile. A minority had carried out the revolution in 1931 and was eschewing peaceful action effectually ever since. These abstained from the polls. Nevertheless, the party led by Gil Robles did so well that it alone of all parties came back stronger after the election. By all the rules of parliamentary democracy this in itself was a national vote of confidence in the Catholic democrat. The combined parties of the Right polled about a quarter of a million more votes than the parties of the Left. Thus, a majority of the nation was proved to be on the side of Gil Robles. When we add the disappointed abstentionists of the Right, it is clear that the majority was substantial. The left polled its maximum, and its maximum was smaller than the minimum of the Right. Mark that well! The majority of seats, however, owing to unevenness in the constituencies, was taken by the Left. With the larger part of the nation against it, the United Front was able to form a strong Government. This was done. Casares Quiroga, one of the old Pact politicians, became premier. The resolution of this minority to carry its extreme purposes was shown by the deposition of Zamora in favor of an out-and-out Left politician, Azaña, as President. Thus a Left Government won power on a minority vote, and showed at once that it was determined to pursue as extreme a policy as if it had been authorized by the mass of the nation.

V. THE OUTBREAK

A MINORITY Government may be legitimate, and it is the duty of the nation to obey it in all lawful measures. It is morally bound, however, to rule with moderation, to maintain even justice, and not to enact measures that are repugnant to the impotent majority.

The Government of Casares Quiroga was technically legitimate, but who will say that it remained legitimate when it threw aside its obligations? It was, in truth, the creature of its own extremists. The well-known tactics of Bolshevism are to get power into the hands of the Left and then to devour the Left. Weak men who, as Liberals or moderate Socialists, ally themselves with Communists, or seek toleration for Bolshevism make themselves tools of a movement which scoffs at majority rule and democracy and uses them merely as a mask. These men fail to understand the true nature of the ideology. They do not restrain Communism by their moderation, but rather empower it through their cooperation.

This was made clear by Largo Caballero, soon after the erection of the Popular Front Government.[19] He said that the purpose of his friends was to transform the existing regime into a Soviet Republic, but that the moment was not yet ripe. The democratic Republic would be allowed to operate for a time, but the proletariat would put it aside and set up its own dictatorship. "We will choose our own time, but the present does not quite suit us." Six months later, Largo Caballero achieved his end—he became Premier of a Government in the hands of Communism.

That the new Government was heading in this direction was known well to friend and foe. It is the tactics of Bolshevism, once a weak Left Government has been got into power and the Right thus silenced, to make Government by democratic means come to a full stop by means of strikes and disorders. Power can then be seized by the revolutionary intriguers at this stage.

Quickly these tactics were revealed. Strikes, strikes, strikes, were the order of the day. Agitators went through the paralyzed industrial centers, stirring up the mob to violence. Between February and July 1936, in five months of government by the Left minority, these horrible streams of outrages poured over the land. There were 341 strikes, many of them "general strikes" on a massive scale; 411 churches were attacked, and 160 of them were gutted with fire; 43 newspaper offices were raided, and 10 of them destroyed; many churches were closed by revolutionary mayors, and 69 Catholic centers were destroyed.

---

[19] Largo Caballero (1869-1946), a famous Spanish politician, trade unionist, and leader of the Socialist Workers' Party and Workers' General Union. He would serve as Prime Minister in 1936-1937.

Popular Front militias ransacked monasteries and convents, desecrating the tombs of dead religious in Barcelona and elsewhere.

In these proceedings no fewer than 1,556 persons lost their lives, many of them clergy. Read that catalogue of horror; read, too, how Catholic schools and convents were set on fire, and furniture and statues thrown into the street, and how protection was steadily refused to church property. It all happened in five months—supposed to be months of democratic rule. In Parliament, Calvo Sotelo and Gil Robles stood up and read the list of outrages, demanding that the Government afford adequate protection. They were denied their demand. The parties of the Right were mocked. They were taunted with responsibility for deeds done by desperate men, the Fascists who struck back at the terrorists, although (as we have seen) the Right in Parliament had not collaborated with Fascism and had striven to prevent a break-away into that last course of desperation.

The ally of Gil Robles, the high-minded conservative leader Calvo Sotelo—he was an experienced statesman who had been Minister for Finance under Primo de Rivera's fruitful rule, and represented the College of Advocates— complained in Parliament that the Government was refusing him adequate protection from the raging terror. The guards on his house had been changed for strangers, in whom he had no trust. "We'll have your own life!" cried a member of the Left. Calvo Sotelo quoted the words of a Saint: "You may take my life, but my honour is my own." He was refused the protection that he demanded.

A member of the State forces had been shot by some unknown hand. Within a few hours of his vain appeal for protection, Calvo Sotelo was taken from his house and murdered, as a reprisal. The men who arrested him were

THE OUTBREAK

Government servants. He was murdered on the infamous principle that all defenders of the Right were public enemies. On the same night, the house of Gil Robles was visited, presumably by the same murder gang. He was absent, and so escaped. He attended the funeral and denounced the Government under whose aegis his illustrious colleague had been slain. He furthermore spoke bitterly of the obstruction of his own efforts to sustain orderly constitutional rule. The Government had shown itself no Government, but a protector of violence. Then he fled, a marked man whose life was not safe in the capital city of the country that he served. Calvo Sotelo was murdered on July 14. The rule of law was at an end. On July 19, the soldiers struck to quell anarchy by war.

VI. ISSUES AT STAKE: THE LEFT

A SUCCESSION of stop-gap Governments at Madrid yielded to one by Senor Giral, who held power till the city of Irún fell to the rebels early in September. Giral's Government included no Communists, and it was Largo Caballero the Communist who declared by radio that defenders of Madrid were defending democracy: he used the mask of democracy even when he was the master of the situation. It was the Communistic union of which he was head, and the Communist Youth that he founded, which were carrying out the destruction of churches and maintaining the Red Terror at that very time. While Giral was premier, the Red Terror could be represented as loyal measures to defend the State, a plea by which foreigners were led to believe that the revolt was a rebellion against legitimacy.

When, however, Irún fell in September and the victory of the insurgents seemed near, Giral's Government broke up. Largo Caballero became Prime Minister and formed what he had been planning so long: an out-and-out

ISSUES AT STAKE: THE LEFT

Marxist Government. The outer world was not allowed to know whether the stop-gap politicians of Giral's type broke in panic or were coerced. It was enough that they went, and a Government of undisguised Red revolution was established.

The program of Largo Caballero's Government was plain from the men with which he staffed it, even if it were not known by his character and declarations. When he put an atheist in charge of education, he showed his intention to go as far as farthest Russia towards the extinction of Christian order, morality, and belief. It was at the same time that M. Rosenberg, the Russian Ambassador, arrived in Madrid with greetings to President Azaña and was assured by Azaña that Madrid stood for Moscow's principles.

The victory of Madrid, therefore, would involve what has happened in Russia, namely, the destruction of organized Christianity. Churches would be closed everywhere in Spain as they are closed already in Catalonia and wherever else the Reds prevail. This, for Christians, is immeasurably the greatest issue at stake. Beside this contemplated spiritual desolation, the material results of Marxism are small; yet, in themselves, how horrible! The whole land of Spain would be nationalized. Instead of their lot being eased, as a Right victory promises, the peasants would see themselves as a class wiped out altogether and State farms worked by servile labor would be established. This would mean the end of rural joys, rural virtues, rural family life.

Christian marriage and family life would end, as in Russia and the name of God would be forbidden in the schools. Industries would be mechanized, and nationalized on the Russian mass model, so that the small, independent craftsman and shopkeeper would go; and the town population would be made servile. These changes would be brought about by the "dictatorship of the proletariat"; that is, by the ruthless command of men who have no respect for religion, culture, tradition—for any of the spiritual things that sweeten even mortal life.

Art and letters would go the way of the sublime treasures that were destroyed in the three terrors—the terror of 1934, the terror of the peace, and the terror of the war. Non-productive classes, as Marxists choose to regard all save the proletariat, would be impoverished or killed off, as in Russia, where a million people were shot down, largely by Chinese mercenaries. We need not defend the too great inequality of classes to see that the levelling of all society to one class must entail immeasurable cruelty, with true gain to none.

VII. ISSUES AT STAKE: THE RIGHT

WE TURN to the cause of the Right. It is, first and foremost, the salvation of Spain from Russia's plight. Immediately after the beginning of the uprising, General Franco cried to the world that he had risen to save Western civilization in Spain. It is plain that nothing save drastic action could have checked the headlong progress of the Red movement; and, whether Franco acted in the best of ways, or whether he is perfectly sincere—some writers meanly allege that he only wants power—it is a truth beyond yea or nay that Western civilization will perish if he fails.

Victory will mean that the Church will be restored, and that anarchistic agitation will be put down. The rule of authority in some form or another, will be restored. "In what form?" it will be asked. Here we come to a highly important matter, on which it is necessary to be clear and firm: We say first that any form of Government that will secure the freedom of worship to the Catholic population

A church destroyed by the Republican army

and the safety of life and property, will be better than what Spain has endured in the last five years. A pure military Government which achieved these good ends would be so far good. So would a Fascist Government. Yet few of us would favor either of those forms, at any rate for more than an emergency period, and it is natural that our sympathy with the insurgent Generals will be greater if it can be shown that they intend more than to rescue Spain from Bolshevism—that is, if they propose a lasting reform.

ISSUES AT STAKE: THE RIGHT

Now, the first heartening fact is that Gil Robles, after escaping from Madrid and getting to safety in Portugal, went into the liberated part of Spain and made his way to Burgos, where the military Government sits. There he announced his adhesion to the insurgent cause, "nuestro movimiento salvador," to quote his own words to the present writer.[20] The methods were not his—his methods had been tried and had failed—but he stood now with the soldiers. At Seville his friend the great Catholic poet Jose Maria Peman, served the insurgent cause under General Quiepo de Llano.[21]

What is good enough for Spain's greatest democratic statesman and greatest Catholic writer, ought to be good enough to secure the approval of outside observers. The Generals have satisfied these men that they stand for what they have stood for—the regeneration of Spain. If the insurgents win, Gil Robles probably will be called upon to form a civil Government under the Army's protection, like Dr. Salazar in Portugal, and then he will be enabled to carry out the social reforms, drawn in the light of the Encyclicals, which were frustrated under the old regime.[22]

---

[20] "Our saving movement"

[21] José María Pemán y Pemartín (1897-1981) was a journalist and director of the Real Academia de la Lengua, a Spanish royal institution charged with maintaining the stability of the Spanish language. He was an early supporter of Franco and the Falange movement.

[22] Dr. António de Oliveira Salazar (1889-1970), corporatist Catholic dictator of Portugal from 1932 to1968.

VIII. THE WAR DESCRIBED

Let none doubt that the revolt is popular in nature, supported by a broad mass of Spaniards motivated by little else than the security of their property and worship. An Irishman at the insurgent headquarters writes:

> I am beholding the world's greatest racial and religious resurrection, ignored, misrepresented by correspondents whose countries do not want another great Catholic Power to rise.

Here are some passages from an account of the crusading spirit of the insurgents, from the *L'Osservatore Romano*, the Vatican newspaper as translated by *The Standard*:[23]

---

[23] I have been unable to track down the exact date of publication of the *L'Osservatore Romano* article de Blácam quotes here; undoubtedly it comes from late summer 1936 during the early victories of the Francoists.

THE WAR DESCRIBED

Amidst these horrible scenes of blood and fire, destruction, and ruin, it is well to turn our eyes to the splendid reawakening of the religious spirit of the true Spanish people, a reawakening so splendid that it has astonished even the Catholics themselves by its vigor.

While in some parts churches and convents are being razed, in others the crowds may be seen begging pardon of God and praying for victory for the good. While on one side priests and religious are being massacred, on the other their hands are kissed in public as a sign of respect and veneration. While some die cursing God, others go to death with the glorious cry on their lips; "Long live Christ, long life Spain."

We have unquestionable evidence of this new growth of the Catholic spirit in Spain in the present crisis. It consists of authentic actual facts, which have taken place here and there in both the districts where the faith had been preserved in all its strength and those others where it had been suffocated by the Communist propaganda. This is proof that the reawakening is general.

A father of seven, going to enlist, said: "It frightens me to think that these seven children may be deprived of their father; but it would be much more terrible that they should be deprived of their catechism." He fell shortly afterwards, bravely fighting against the Reds. Another workman, a widower with four children, shut up his small shop and entrusted his children to the neighbors that he might go to fight.

Four brothers, the sons of a widow, decided to go to the front to take part in the war against the Reds. As they did not wish to leave their mother completely derelict, one of them consented to remain at home with her. However, when the good woman heard that one of the sons was to remain with her, she angrily told him that she would refuse to give him food if he dared to remain at home while his brothers were fighting for the Faith.

Correspondents in Pamplona write: "What a wonderful sight these youths are. How joyous they are. It is a pleasure to see them with the Sacred Heart badge on their breasts. Some of them wear the Brown Scapular or Child of Mary medals. One night twenty priests were kept busy hearing confessions in the soldiers' quarters. Many made their confessions on the sidewalks or under the trees in the public squares, kneeling down in public to receive absolution. All this is, as it were, a strong injection of faith into the army, which stood in need of it. When the men go to enlist they sing songs such as this: "Weep not mother, weep not that I take up arms. The body is of no value, that which has value is the soul." In Salamanca the

THE WAR DESCRIBED

whole population has recourse to God. An indescribable enthusiasm has been manifested there. The churches are full. Even boys between the ages of 10 and 16 offer themselves as volunteers.

A commandant who received some medals of the Sacred Heart for his troops expressed pleasure at the gift and said that he prayed much that they would do their best at the front. "But" he added, "the non-combatants must help with their prayers, for prayer not only comforts the soul, but it strengthens the body."

From Cadiz we hear that there is a consoling religious reaction, "Long live Christ the King," is heard shouted in the streets, in the very city where formerly so many blasphemies were heard, and God's name was so often insulted and profaned. The ringing of the Angelus has been introduced, and it is an edifying sight to see the soldiers halt, even in the streets, to recite the prayer in which the civilians also join. On the day when this practice was introduced, the general reminded the soldiers that it was a salutation addressed to the Blessed Virgin. He recalled the history of its institution, and he himself recited it with the soldiers. Many of those present were moved to tears.

In Seville the populace and the soldiers show their respect and veneration for the priests not only in the churches but in the streets also. The number of those who frequent the Sacrament is remarkable.

At Murcia a professor was assassinated in the church of Tribaldos because he had always been an ardent defender of the Catholic cause. This is how one of his brothers communicated the news to another brother: "Mother and sister-in-law have borne this great sorrow with a truly admirable fortitude. Don't you worry. We are prepared to suffer whatever God may send us, for it is an honour for the family to have a martyr, and that is what our brother is, having bravely defended the cause of Christ all his life."

At Badajoz as soon as the insurgents entered the city the churches were immediately filled to offer thanks to God for delivery from the tyranny and from extermination."

The foregoing examples are but a few leaves from the book of Spain's new Crusade. How grand was that moment when the insurgent forces, having captured Valladolid after the Red terror had sacked the churches, had Mass said in the public place, with military honors, for the assembled city! How happily did 100,000 people of Saragossa march in procession when a Red aeroplane dropped on the shrine of Our Lady of the Pillar bombs that failed to explode, and one of Spain's most treasured relics, the miraculous image of Our Lady was saved!

IX. WHAT IS FASCISM?

IT MAY be said here that all this religious fervor is fine, but that outside sympathizers cannot approve of the political intentions of the Nationalist Generals. They may liberate religion (which is the great thing, after all), but they announce that they will set up a lasting military Government and will suppress trade unions and Parliamentary rule. They are what the Communists call Fascists. How can this be squared with liberty?

We must define Fascism. This system began in Italy in 1922, and its inventor, Mussolini, truly said that it was not for export—that it belonged peculiarly to the Italian people in their present time of national exaltation. Three things exist in Italy which are bulked as Fascism: (i) the dictatorship of one of the most popular national leaders of history (as we must describe him in truth, whether we approve of him or not); (ii) Fascism, or the control of the State by an armed political party; and (iii) the corporative economic system, by which the industries of the nation are conducted by guilds of men and masters instead of by State industry as under Socialism, or by big financiers opposed by trade unions as in pure Capitalistic countries.

Now, any of these three things could exist separately. In Portugal, the corporative system exists, but not Fascism. It is Portugal that the Spanish leaders have cited as their model. In point of fact, therefore, the Spanish movement is not Fascist. Among the parties of the Right who have united under the Patriot flag, the Fascists are but one group—a very heroic group, let us add, which has poured out its young blood for the nation.

The Spanish "salvation"—to employ a term which Gil Robles has used in a letter to the present writer—is largely inspired by the splendid recovery of Portugal in recent years. Like Spain, Portugal was exhausted three hundred years ago and recovered in our own days. Following half a century of struggle and revolution, and the fall of the monarchy, a Catholic soldier, General Carmona, set up a military Government with national approval in 1926. After two years, he called in a philosopher-statesman, the almost monastic scholar, Dr. Oliveira Salazar, to act as reconstructor of the State. Poor, a lover of his village and true son of the rural culture, Salazar set out to multiply small owners and to base the State on freemen. He organized the industries on the "corporative" system but avoided the Italian method which makes them part of the political system. He set up a popular legislature, with half its representation professional. Above all, he made religion and patriotism, order and peace, his principles. He took Catholic philosophy for his guide and the Social Encyclicals for his texts.

Under the protection of the military chief of State, this new Portuguese Constitution has worked wonderfully well. Prosperity has returned to the land. Privilege has been suppressed. The health of the nation is reflected in a spiritual revival which the Cardinal Patriarch of Lisbon described in 1936 as "a miracle." That is the example of what authority can do, when directed by Catholic idealism and principle. The example of Portugal may be denounced as "Fascism" by unscrupulous enemies; but no honest man can say that it is ignoble, or that it is an attack on true liberty.

The mind which thinks that there can be no liberty save where the English Parliamentary system is maintained is easily misled by the cry of "Fascism," but it makes two vital blunders: (i) the English system is held by such sound English democrats as the late G. K. Chesterton to be undemocratic, since it leaves power in the hands of a Press-controlling oligarchy and goes with an order that allows only 7 per cent of the nation to own property; and (ii) the Communists are themselves contemptuous of Parliament, so that their victory over the "Fascists" will not save it.

Mark this: that these Latin nations have been leaders of civilization in the past and when they devise a new system, it is likely at least to deserve study by thoughtful outsiders. The Portuguese system, let it be repeated, is a free, enlightened system that does away with class war, that evil thing for which countries nearer home have not yet found a cure.

X. SOME CHARGES ANSWERED

IT IS NOT our purpose to pin our absolute approval on the ideals or the methods of the insurgents; it is for Spaniards to find their own solution to their own problems. Our purpose is simply to vindicate the insurgent cause from the charges made against it (i) that it is a mere outbreak of military tyranny; (ii) that it means that Catholicism is repressive, and (iii) that the Red cause is a just cause, or the Red outrages justly provoked by Catholicism.

We will answer some points on which defenders of the Red lay great stress. (i) *General Franco brought Moorish troops into Europe, to make war on white men.*—This is a sad truth. Franco struck with the weapon at his hand, the professional army of the State, which includes Moors and legionaries. None can be glad that Spain, like France and Britain, has used dusky troops in Europe. Yet, four points must be noted:

(a) Whereas the mob armed by the Reds looted and massacred non-combatants, no such charge is made against

SOME CHARGES ANSWERED

Franco's troops—they bore themselves as true disciplined soldiers. Regular troops under professional command are far less dangerous to non-combatants than hastily enrolled, unseasoned volunteers, who so easily lose their heads under fire.

(b) The actual part taken in the war by the Moors and legionaries is much less than the hostile press has pretended. The bulk of the army is native Spanish.

(c) To the Flag flocked hosts of enthusiastic youths and elders who have been trained during the progress of the war and are being used increasingly.

(d) Complaints against disciplined Moors, even if they took a bigger part than they have taken, ought to die on the lips of Communists, seeing that the Russian Bolsheviks used Chinese mercenaries to do their work of terrorism and to perform the massacres of thousands of Russian Christians.

(ii) *Franco's men shot their prisoners after victory, and especially at Badajoz killed many hundreds.*—This also is deplorably true. Both sides in this hideous civil war have shot their prisoners. The Reds began it, by slaughtering all fighting men who surrendered. The huge executions at Badajoz were a terrible military reprisal, done, it may be added, when a city was captured in which the Reds had massacred priests, crucifying some of them. The act of reprisal was a fearful punishment, and it is recalled how many of the prisoners to be executed asked for priests, whom only the victors could supply, and happily went to God in penitence, with absolution—the happiest fate that could befall men whose hands had been dipped in innocent blood. Further, the executions were done only after trial,

FOR GOD AND SPAIN

Moorish troops from Morocco fought for Franco during the Spanish Civil War.

and only persons proved to have shared in the outrages were put to death.

The ruthlessness of the Spanish war is not new. In former wars of liberation, the same awful extremes were seen, as when El Cid Campeador wrought a terrible punishment on Valentia, and the gentle Queen Isabella of Castile on the violent rebels of her day. Spain's mixture of blood since the Arab and Moor invasions has left a heritage of extremism that shocks us. Franco's vengeance has been commensurate with the terror that it punishes and seeks to prevent from recurrence. If we found our priests crucified, would we be less wrathful, less stern than he? Let us pray, however, that mercy will temper the victory of the Right, and let our influence be used with the victors to be moderate and so to lift Spain from its present bloody misery. If we lend moral support to the cause of the Right, we have a right to be heard in pleading for mercy; but not if we justify or palliate the Red Terror.

(iii) *The Church in Spain was corrupt, rich, sluggish, tyrannical.*—Suppose this to be true, is it a way to reform a Church to burn it and abolish moral law? However, the charge is false. When the Church in Spain has given hundreds of martyrs to God in a few weeks—when its bishops, priests, nuns and pious laity have suffered cheerfully and unflinchingly for the name of Christ in such hosts—who dares deny the Church admiration and reverence? The Spanish Church is a Church of martyrs, sublime in this age of indifference. As to its riches, its parochial clergy were amongst the poorest in Europe; and its treasures were confiscated two years ago. The Orders that suffered most were those that were pouring forth energy and learning and piety on works of education, as when the magnificent Jesuit Institute, that trained poor boys to be engineers and craftsmen—and was the premier technical institute of all Spain—was destroyed in the name of the Republic.

(iv) *Spain has the highest proportion of illiteracy in Europe.*—This is a charge against the old regime and against the Republic which allowed Church schools to be destroyed and suppressed the teaching Orders; not against the reformers now in arms. Further, it is a charge that involves a lot of misunderstanding. A man able to read, who reads shoddy and lying newspapers, is not really better educated than an illiterate who has a fine traditional culture around him. While Spain had many illiterates, it also has a lofty national culture. Its newspapers are the best in Europe and are written by scholars. In Spain, an ill-educated man soon finds himself among his betters. The Catholic philosophy is accessible to all, which is not the case in the babel of some nations.

(v) *The Church and the old regime did nothing to end the landlord system under which Spanish farmers suffered.—* The Spanish landlord system was totally unlike what we understand by landlordism. It was sluggish, and needed reform, but Gil Robles, the principal leader of the Right, was the one statesman who set out to reform it. There is no hope of reform in the Left; for the efforts to socialize the land actually drove much of it out of cultivation. Furthermore, the old regime and its faults are things of the past. Franco and Gil Robles are not defenders of the old regime. They are champions of a new, reformed regime. The faults of the past are not chargeable to them. The people of rural Spain rallied to the insurgent cause, showing that they themselves regard the patriots as deliverers.

(vi) *The insurgents intend to suppress trade unions.—* They may suppress the revolutionary unions which have carried out the Marxist program of violence. These unions have nothing in common with the unions that we know. The alleged intention to suppress unions can apply only to the Anarchist and Communist bodies, as the Christian unions are supporting the patriot cause. With guilds of masters and men formed on the Portuguese model, unions for class war would be absurd.

(vii) *The insurgents want to restore the Monarchy, with which it is admitted that so much fault can be found.—* The monarchy is for the Spanish people to restore if they so choose; that is, if they believe that this institution,

SOME CHARGES ANSWERED

associated with the past glories of Spain, still has merit in it. There is no intention to restore Alfonso XIII, whose mistakes and, doubtless, faults did much harm; but his son Don Juan would make a clean fresh start if the nation recalled him. However, the patriot generals have affirmed that they are not fighting for the monarchy. Their head, General Cabanellas, is a life-long Republican.[24] When Don Juan offered to serve the cause at Burgos, his offer was declined, and he was told that the question of the monarchy must be left to the decision of the nation when freedom and order have been re-established. Here we have another parallel to Portugal, where there are divided opinions as to whether the national recovery should be put under a restored monarchy, and the rulers of new Portugal have replied that the issue must be left until reconstruction is complete and a free national decision can be taken. Late in September, one insurgent leader was reported in the Roman Press to have said that the monarchy would be recalled in the end, at the people's demand, as a means to unite the regional groups, to which local powers would be given. If Spain wants its King, hail to him!

---

[24] General Miguel Cabanellas Ferrer (1872-1938) was a Freemason and president of the National Defense Junta that proclaimed Francisco Franco head of government and Generalissimo on September 21, 1936–though Cabanellas was the only one who dissented to this choice. He served as the Chief Inspector of the Army under Franco until his death.

XI. WHAT IS OUR PART?

WE HAVE proved our case. We have shown that the chivalry of Spain struck when arms only could avail. The sublime heroism of the Alcazar does not come from men with a selfish cause. Spain rises to save her Faith and her freedom, and when she wins she will lead in the grand revival of Catholic civilization, now, please God, at hand.

For us, who are not Spaniards, but who are fellow-Christians and citizens of a common western civilization, remembering that all Christian countries are rightly provinces of one grand Catholic commonwealth, what happens in Spain is of vital brotherly consequence. We are not called upon to defend all that is done by those with whom we sympathize, and the form of Government for which they are striving is their own concern; but it is our duty to understand their case and to defend them from slander. We must share their anxiety that, under some form, Christian order shall be restored.

To this end, though we cannot give material aid, we do not forget how Spain sent us ships and armies and gave colleges to educate our priests and leading laymen in our

WHAT IS OUR PART?

own dark hour. We can give, however, spiritual and intellectual aid; in the first place by our prayers, as our prelates direct and exhort us, and secondly by combating the false charges laid against our brother Catholics, now suffering or in arms, also by giving wise counsel and keeping our own house in order as an example and strength to our neighbor.

Were we to stand neutral or indifferent, when this Last Crusade is being fought, we would deserve to go down to history as a shameless generation, helping by our silence and consent the new Crucifixion. Hear, then, the words of Rome:

> In the parts of Spain where the Red Terror reigns triumphant [says *L'Osservatore Romano*] thousands of martyrs die for Christ, just as in the early ages of the Church. Many other heroic acts of the Christians show that after twenty centuries the Faith has the same invincible strength, even though the persecutors have become ever more ferocious. The time will come when they, too, will be forced to exclaim: "Thou has conquered, O Galilean."

APPENDIX

HIS HOLINESS the Pope, from his summer residence, Castel Gandolfo Monday, 14th September, 1936, broadcast to the world a striking address which he delivered to 500 Spanish refugees, including Bishops and Priests and Nuns. From the Holy Father's moving address we give the following extracts.

The tragic happenings in Spain speak to Europe and the whole world and proclaim once more to what extent the foundations of all order, of all culture, of all civilization are being menaced. This menace, it must be added, is all the more serious, more persistent, and more active by reason of a profound ignorance and a disclaiming of the Truth— by reason of the truly satanic hatred against God and against humanity, redeemed by Him, in all that concerns Religion and the Catholic Church.

This point has been so often admitted and, as We just observed, openly confessed that it is superfluous for Us to speak on the matter further when the events of Spain have spoken with such an appalling eloquence. It is opportune and even necessary, and for Us a duty, to warn all against the insidiousness with which the heralds of the forces of perversion are seeking to find some common ground for a possible approach and collaboration on the part of Catholics, and this on the basis of a distinction between ideology and application between ideas and action between the economic and moral orders.

This insidiousness is dangerous in the extreme, and its purpose is purely and simply to deceive and disarm Europe and the world in favor of an unfailing program of hate, perversion, and destruction, by which they are being threatened. Another truth is that, with this renewed revelation and open confession of hate for religion and the Catholic Church, so obvious in Spain, a further lesson is being offered to Europe and the world, a lesson precious and highly salutary for all who do not care to close their eyes and grope in the dark.

Now, at last, it is certain and obvious from the very confession of these forces of perversion which are currently threatening everything and everybody that the one real obstacle in their way is Christian teaching and the consistent practice of Christian living, as these are taught and enjoyed by the Catholic religion and the Catholic Church.

Wherever and with whatever means, insidious or violent and according to circumstances, and with whatever fictitious and insincere distinctions between the Catholic Church and religious politics, difficulties, obstacles, and barriers are placed in the way of the full development of the position and influence of the Catholic religion and the Catholic Church, with its Divine mandate and authority, precisely to that extent there is aided and abetted the pernicious action of the forces of perversion.

This is not the first time that We have set forth these very grave considerations, and have recommended them to all, particularly to those in positions of responsibility. In this matter there is no testimony more authoritative than yours, because you, in your person and in what you hold most dear, your Fatherland, have experienced the evil disaster which is threatening us all.

It has recently been asserted that the Catholic Church and the Catholic religion have shown themselves unprepared and ineffective in the face of such evil disasters, and the example of Spain—and not merely Spain—has been urged in proof of this. Very much to the point in this matter is a reflection of Alexander Manzoni: "There is no need to have recourse to examples to justify the Church; it is enough to look at Her teaching."[25]

The observation is no less obvious than solid and profound. We want a society in which there is a genuinely free and untrammeled opportunity for the teachings which the Church and the Catholic Religion unfailingly inculcate with the force of law and essential direction, willed by God as a norm for individual conduct and dignity, for private, public, professional and social justice and for the sanctity of the family, teachings on the origin and exercise of authority in other spheres, on human brotherhood lifted to a Divine level, in Christ and His Mystical Body, the Church,

---

[25] Alexander Manzoni (1785-1873). Italian poet, novelist, and philosopher. Manzoni was both a devout Catholic and proponent of Italian unification. He was admired by Pius XI, who also quoted in his encyclical *Divini Illius Magistri*, calling Manzoni "an excellent writer and at the same time a profound and conscientious thinker."

WHAT IS OUR PART?

His Holiness Pope Pius XI (1922-1939)

on the dignity of labor as a Divine undertaking of redemption, looking to an assured reward, teachings on the obligations of mutual charity, of which the sole rule and criterion is the good, and the needs of our neighbor, as these are felt and measured in love, which can have no bounds, as it is like the love to which God Himself has a right.

We want a society in which there is full and undisputed influence and authority of His teachings and those other principles, theoretical and practical, organically related to these teachings, and we ask how and by what means can the Church and the Catholic Religion make a greater and better contribution to the real well-being, whether of the individual or the family or society? Certainly a heavy and formidable responsibility lies on all those who, by reason of and in proportion to the character of their office, fail to oppose to these great evils every remedy and barrier that is possible.

We know only too well that there are many other grave obstacles in the various fields of public, private, collective, and individual life which are opposed to the full efficacy and efficiency, influence, and action, of the Catholic religion and Catholic Church. We must, however, content Ourselves with the indications We have just set forth in order not to delay any further that Fatherly and Apostolic Benediction which you have come to ask of the Common Father at the Throne of the Vicar of Christ. The benediction, beloved sons, which you are asking to receive, and which your Father is longing to bestow, a benediction which you have more than merited. We have willed and so disposed our choice to greet far and wide your brothers

WHAT IS OUR PART?

suffering in exile who have wanted but in vain to be with you this day.

There is a disposition of Divine Providence which has willed you to be in many places, scattered far and wide, so that you, who bear the mark of the tragic events which have afflicted you in your dear Spain and Our Spain, may bear personal testimony of the heroic attachments to the Faith of your Fathers, to the Faith which by hundreds and thousands has added Confessors and Martyrs to the already glorious Martyrology of the Church.

And this, We learn, with inexplicable consolation, which has been the occasion for an intensive and devout renewal and wide awakening of Christian life, particularly among the good, simple people of Spain, and which heralds the dawn and beginning of fairer days for the whole of Spain. To all this, good and faithful people, to all this dear and noble Spain which has suffered so much, We direct Our Benediction, with the desire that it may reach them, and to them, no less, Our daily prayers go out and will continue to go out, until peace finally returns. Our Benediction, above any political or mundane consideration, goes out, in a special manner, to all those who have assumed the difficult and dangerous task of defending and restoring the rights and honour of God and religion, to save the rights and dignity of conscience, the condition and most sound base of all human and civil well-being. Their task, We have said, is both difficult and dangerous, for it is only too easy for the daily ardor and difficulty of defense to go to lengths which are not fully warranted, and further intentions, less pure and selfish interests and mere party feelings, may easily enter to cloud and change the morality and responsibility of what is being done.

Our fatherly heart can never forget, and in this moment more than ever it must recall, with the most sincere and fatherly gratitude, all those who with purity of intention and unselfish motives have sought to intervene in the interests of humanity, and Our gratitude is not diminished even though we have had to realize the failure of their noble efforts.

And what of the others? What is to be said of all those others who are also, and never ceased to be, Our sons, in spite of the deeds and persecutions so odious and so cruel to persons and things to Us so dear and sacred. What of those who, as far as distance permitted, have not even spared Our Person, and who with expressions and gesture so highly offensive have treated Us not as sons with a father, but as soldiers with an enemy who is particularly hated.

We have, beloved sons, Divine precepts and examples which may seem too difficult for poor and unaided human nature to obey and imitate, but which are in reality, with Divine grace, beautiful and attractive to the Christian soul and to your souls, beloved sons, so that We cannot for one moment doubt what is left for Us to do—to love them, and to love them with a special love born of mercy and compassion.

We love and think we can do nothing else than pray for them—to pray that the serene vision of truth will illuminate their minds and will reopen their hearts to the desire in fraternal love for the real common good. We pray that they may return to The Father, who awaits them with longing and will make a joyous festival of their return.

We pray that they may be one with us when shortly— of this we have full confidence in Almighty God—the rainbow of peace will shine forth in the clear sky of Spain,

WHAT IS OUR PART?

sending the news of peace to the whole of your great and splendid country, of a peace, let Us add, serene in fixture, consoling all sorrows, repairing all harm, contenting every just and wise aspiration, which is compatible with the common good, and heralding a future of order and tranquility, of prosperity with honor.

www.ingramcontent.com/pod-product-compliance
Lightning Source LLC
Chambersburg PA
CBHW051702040426
42446CB00009B/1263